THE GOLDEN YEARS OF RAILROADING

BURLINGTON ROUTE ACROSS THE HEARTLAND

Everywhere West from Chicago

JEFF WILSON

KALMBACH BOOKS

98 99 00 01 02 03 04 05 06 07   10 9 8 7 6 5 4 3 2 1

This product is a Print on Demand format of the original book published by Kalmbach Publishing Company.

For more information, visit our website at http://www.kalmbach.com

On the Cover: An A-B set of unique-to-the-Burlington E5s leads train No. 17, the westbound *California Zephyr*, around the curve at Clarendon Hills, Illinois, in August 1950. The stainless-steel-sheathed diesels were substituting for the F3s normally assigned to the train. Photo by Robert Milner.

Book design: Sabine Beaupré
Cover design: Kristi Ludwig
Map, page 7: John Signor

Publisher's Cataloging-in-Publication
(Provided by Quality Books, Inc.)

Wilson, Jeff.
    Burlington Route across the heartland, everywhere west from Chicago / Jeff Wilson. — 1st ed.
        p.   cm. — (Golden years of railroading)
    Includes index.
    ISBN: 0-89024-337-9

    1. Burlington Northern Railroad Company. 2. Railroads—United States. I. Title. II. Series.

TF25.B8W55 1998   385′.0973
                                     QBI98-673

Contents

An A-B set of unique-to-the-Burlington E5s leads train No. 17, the westbound *California Zephyr,* around the curve at Clarendon Hills, Illinois, in August 1950. The stainless-steel-sheathed diesels were substituting for the F3s normally assigned to the train. Photo by Robert Milner.

A Brief History of the Chicago, Burlington & Quincy Railroad

Everywhere West was an appropriate slogan for a railroad that at one time operated more than 12,000 route-miles across the western United States. However, like many large things, the Burlington Route had humble beginnings.

The roots of what became the Chicago, Burlington & Quincy began in 1850 as the Aurora Branch Railroad, a 12-mile line extending from Aurora (about 38 miles west of Chicago) north to Turner Junction (now West Chicago). Two years later the line had stretched 45 miles westward from Aurora to Mendota, and the railroad's name was changed to the Chicago & Aurora.

The railroad continued its westward expansion, reaching Galesburg in 1854 and the Mississippi River in 1855, the same year the name was changed to the Chicago, Burlington & Quincy Railroad.

In 1864 the Burlington completed its own line into Chicago from Aurora, bypassing the old Galena & Chicago Union connection. This million-dollar project turned the original 12-mile line into a branch, but it gave the Burlington a direct route into Chicago, which became—and remains—a vital link for the railroad.

The CB&Q reached west across the prairies to Lincoln, Nebraska, in 1870 and Denver in 1882. In the meantime the Burlington, in the form of the Chicago, Burlington & Northern, completed a line heading north up the Mississippi to the Twin Cities of Minneapolis and St. Paul, Minnesota, in 1886. The Q officially absorbed the CB&N in 1899.

A defining moment in the Burlington's history came in 1901 when the Northern Pacific and Great Northern together bought 98 percent of the CB&Q's stock. The Great Northern's James J. Hill saw the Burlington as a key connection to Chicago from the Twin Cities as well as an important ally across the western plains. Later that year Hill acquired control of the Northern Pacific, creating the "Hill family" of railroads: the GN, NP, and CB&Q.

In 1908 the Burlington acquired control of the Colorado & Southern and Fort Worth & Denver. This gave the Q a line running south and southwest of Denver through Dallas and, via the Burlington–Rock Island, to Galveston, Texas, on the Gulf of Mexico.

Burlington steam power

Through the teens and twenties the Burlington relied heavily on 2-8-2 Mikados to pull most of its key freight trains. Starting in 1910, the railroad acquired 383 Mikados; many lasted well into the 1950s on branch and secondary assignments. Other notable freight locomotives were the 86 big 2-10-2 engines used primarily on the southern Illinois coal lines. For passenger trains of the early 1900s, the Q had acquired 145 Pacific (4-6-2) locomotives, with 21 heavier 4-8-2s for long-distance trains.

Modern steam locomotives arrived on the CB&Q in 1930. Baldwin delivered eight class O-5 4-8-4 Northerns for use on fast freights. They performed very well, and the Q's West Burlington shops turned out 13 more in 1937, followed by 15 additional improved O-5A Northerns in 1938 and 1940. On the passenger side, 12 4-6-4 Hudsons (Nos. 3000–3011) arrived from Baldwin in 1930. These were also outstanding performers and could be found hauling the Q's name passenger trains throughout the '30s.

Zephyrs

The Burlington became synonymous with its *Zephyrs*, among the most famous fleets of passenger trains in the country. *Zephyrs* were known for their fluted stainless-steel exteriors as well as for speed, luxury, and performance.

The diesel-powered *Pioneer Zephyr*—originally simply the Burlington *Zephyr*—started it all in 1934 as a way of cutting losses on short-run steam-powered trains. The silver three-car train was a huge success and spawned a fleet of *Zephyrs* that covered almost the entire Burlington system.

The Q pioneered the concept of the dome car. The first was the home-built Silver Dome in 1945. It was followed by the Budd-built Vista-Dome cars for the new 1947 *Twin Zephyrs* and many additional trains through the mid-1950s.

Diesels

The Burlington was an early user of diesel power, beginning with the *Zephyrs* in 1934, diesel switchers in the late 1930s and early 1940s, and the unique-to-the-Q stainless-steel E5 passenger engines. The railroad acquired 64 of Electro-Motive's pioneering FT diesels in 1944 and followed that with hundreds of F3 and F7 cab units, as well as four- and six-axle EMD road switchers.

Electro-Motive was a partner in developing the *Pioneer Zephyr*, and the Burlington remained true to EMD—with the exception of a few Baldwin and Alco switchers acquired during World War II—until it bought six U25Bs from General Electric in 1964.

Burlington Northern

From the time the Northern Pacific and Great Northern acquired control of the CB&Q in 1901, the intention had been to merge the three railroads. In fact, in 1930 the Interstate Commerce Commission authorized the GN and NP to merge on the condition that they relinquish control of the Burlington. However, the CB&Q was too valuable a connection for the NP and GN, so the railroads withdrew the merger application in 1931.

A new merger application was filed in 1960, with the Spokane, Portland & Seattle (owned by the GN and NP) added to the mix. After several years of review the merger was finally approved, and on March 2, 1970, the Chicago, Burlington & Quincy became part of the Burlington Northern.

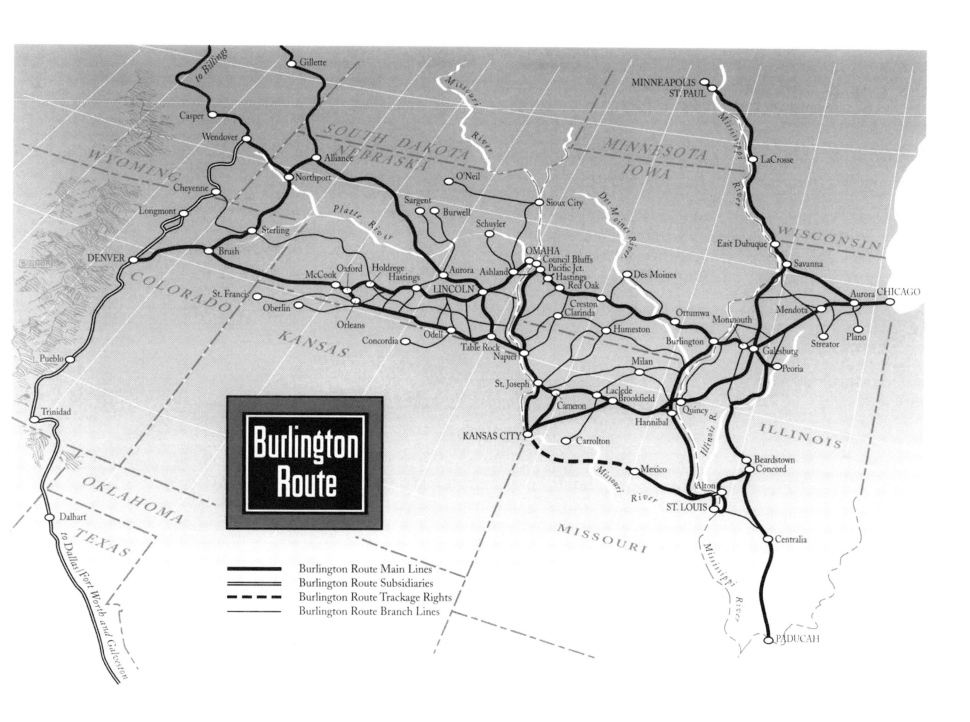

Burlington Route

Burlington Route Main Lines
Burlington Route Subsidiaries
Burlington Route Trackage Rights
Burlington Route Branch Lines

Train No. 18, the inbound *California Zephyr*, backs into Chicago's Union Station following its run from the West Coast on Aug. 21, 1950. Photo by Wallace W. Abbey.

ACROSS THE HEARTLAND

Chicago earned its reputation as the nation's railroad capital in the 1800s, and throughout the 1940s and '50s the Burlington did its part to keep Chicago in the forefront. The Q operated more than 30 passenger trains a day in and out of Chicago's Union Station, which it shared with the Milwaukee Road, the Pennsylvania Railroad, and the Gulf, Mobile & Ohio.

From Chicago the Q sent passenger trains to the West Coast (*California Zephyr* and the earlier *Exposition Flyer*), Denver (*Denver Zephyr*), and St. Paul (*Twin Cities Zephyrs*), as well as many midwestern and western cities.

In addition, the Burlington carried passenger trains of Hill family railroads Great Northern (*Empire Builder* and *Western Star*) and Northern Pacific (*North Coast Limited* and *Mainstreeter*) between Chicago and the Twin Cities.

Suburban territory

The first 38 miles of the Burlington main line west of Chicago to Aurora had three main tracks and more than earned the nickname "racetrack." With a heavy schedule of commuter trains (about 14 inbound trains into Union each morning), at least a dozen intercity passenger trains each way, and a full schedule of freight trains, the racetrack was one busy stretch of railroad.

The commuter trains became known as "dinkies," and the morning and afternoon rushes were known as the dinky parades. Dispatchers had their hands full threading freights and long-distance passenger trains through the rush of commuter trains.

Through the 1950s commuter trains featured rebuilt heavyweight coaches painted green with a tan car-length window area. In 1950 the railroad bought 30 new stainless-steel double-deck gallery cars and added another 30 by the mid-1950s.

Pacific (4-6-2) steam locomotives were typical commuter train power into the 1940s. Diesels began appearing around 1940—first the stainless-steel E5s, then E7s, E8s, and E9s after World War II. The last steam-powered commuter train ran in September 1952.

The diesels assigned to the dinkies were not used strictly in suburban service, but were rotated onto commuter runs in between distance-train assignments. The Q was known for efficient locomotive utilization, and it was common for an E to come in on a name train in the morning, haul a commuter train out and back, then depart on another intercity train in the afternoon or evening.

Denver

This Colorado city at the foot of the Rocky Mountains was the western terminus of the Q's cross-country main line. It was an important link to the West for the Burlington because the

Denver & Rio Grande Western provided a route through the Rockies for the *California Zephyr* as well as many carloads of freight.

The Burlington subsidiary Colorado & Southern stretched south from Denver, linking with the Fort Worth & Denver to provide a line to Dallas and Fort Worth, Texas, and then to the Gulf of Mexico via the Burlington–Rock Island.

The C&S also extended north of Denver to Wendover, Wyoming, where the Burlington proper then continued to Billings, Montana, providing the CB&Q with a valuable connection to the Pacific Northwest via the Northern Pacific and Great Northern.

Denver was home to a major shop for CB&Q and Colorado & Southern locomotives. The massive complex, built in 1923, served locomotives of the both railroads, and was known as both the Joint Shops and the New Shops. Unlike West Burlington, the Denver facility didn't build new locomotives but performed routine repairs, as well as some major rebuilding (mainly before 1930) and conversion projects.

As diesels took over for steam in the 1940s, the need for a major shop facility in Denver decreased, and the shops closed for good in September 1955.

Passengers walk along a platform at Chicago's Union Station in front of E8 No. 9945A.
Photo by William A. Akin, August 1955.

Before the *California Zephyr* captivated the public in 1949, the *Exposition Flyer* carried passengers to San Francisco. The Burlington handed the train—shown here departing Union Station—to the Rio Grande in Denver, which in turn gave it to the Western Pacific at Salt Lake City for the final leg to the West Coast. CB&Q photo, January 28, 1946.

The Great Northern outfitted its streamlined *Empire Builder* with new equipment in June 1951. Here a pair of Q E8s backs the new train set into Union Station in preparation for its first westbound run as a Baldwin switcher makes up the new *Western Star,* which utilized the former *Builder* equipment. Photo by Wallace W. Abbey, June 3, 1951.

The *Denver Zephyr* awaits its next call at the Chicago coach yard on June 3, 1951. Photo by Wallace W. Abbey.

A group of E units await their next assignments at the Zephyr Pit, the Burlington's diesel facility at the 14th Street Coach Yard. Photo by William A. Akin, August 1955.

Cicero Yard on the western outskirts of Chicago was an important gateway for the railroad and was pushing its capacity by the mid-1950s. The Burlington's solution in 1957 and 1958 was to rebuild Cicero from a flat classification yard to a hump yard with electronically controlled retarders and the most modern signal and control equipment available. The 2.3-mile-long yard could then classify up to 3,600 cars per day. Here (above), looking west, a string of cars at right moves up the hump. Looking the other way (left), a boxcar rolls down the hump toward the classification tracks under the Laramie Avenue bridge.
CB&Q photos.

The Burlington's Chicago diesel shops were at Clyde. Electro-Motive FT No. 109 was less than two years old when it was in for a checkup in this February 1946 view. CB&Q photo.

SUBURBAN TERRITORY

Class S-1A Pacific (4-6-2) steam locomotive No. 2820 brings an outbound commuter train past Harlem Ave. in June 1936. Note the old streetcar track in the street at the crossing. Photo by L. E. Griffith.

Just west of Riverside the Q crossed over the Des Plaines River. Here two E7s lead a string of heavyweight equipment across the bridge. Photo by John D. Weidenfeller.

A three-unit set of F3s leads the westbound *California Zephyr* on the center track past an inbound commuter train led by an E8. The trains are passing over the Indiana Harbor Belt tracks at La Grange. Photo by Robert Milner, May 1950.

Departing passengers head for home as the conductor gives a highball to a commuter train at La Grange. The double-deck commuter cars first appeared in 1950. Photo by Melvin N. Patrick.

A crossing guard earns his keep as the Vista-Dome-equipped *California Zephyr* rolls through La Grange behind passenger F3s on May 30, 1950. Photo by James G. LaVake.

The local freight out of Aurora, led this August 1950 day by NW2 No. 9222, pulls cars out of the freight house siding at La Grange. This train originated in Aurora each morning and worked local industries to Morton Park, returning to Aurora in the afternoon. Photo by Robert Milner.

An outbound dinky passes a pair of steam locomotives stored on a spur at La Grange on April 2, 1951.
Photo by Bob Borcherding.

Shovelnose diesels put in occasional appearances on commuter trains. Here No. 9907A, Silver Knight, originally built for the *Denver Zephyr* in 1936, totes an eastbound dinky with conventional equipment near La Grange in August 1950. The 1,800-hp locomotive would be converted to a B unit less than a year later and cut up for scrap in 1955. Photo by Robert Milner.

Stone Avenue Station, at milepost 14.14, was just four-tenths of a mile west of the La Grange station. Here the west-bound *Exposition Flyer* passes inbound commuter train No. 222 on Feb. 15, 1948, at 1:47 p.m. Photo by Robert Milner.

Steam could be found in suburban service through the 1940s, as shown by Pacific No. 2864 powering a Chicago-bound dinky past Highlands in July 1946. Photo by L. E. Griffith.

The fireman on an outbound E unit had this view of a Chicago-bound commuter train easing to a stop at Hinsdale in August 1955. Photo by William A. Akin.

An E5A and B lead the heavyweight equipment of the eastbound *Ak-sar-ben Zephyr* through Westmont in July 1946. Photo by L. E. Griffith.

Twenty years before it would gain fame by pulling several steam farewell fan-trip runs, Mikado No. 4960 cruises through Downers Grove with a string of refrigerator cars on April 23, 1941. The 2-8-2 was built in 1923 by Baldwin. Photo by Ted Gay.

Before suburbia sprawled to connect the towns west of Chicago, the sweeping curve at Naperville was a great place to watch trains. Here a matched set of EMD F3s rolls toward Chicago in September 1950. Photo by Bob Borcherding.

A single E7 leads the articulated trainset of the westbound *Nebraska Zephyr* around the Naperville curve in September 1950. Photo by Bob Borcherding.

A westbound freight led by F3 No. 133A pauses to do some early-morning switching at Naperville.
Photo by Dean M. Givler.

Brand-new four-unit FT No. 100, with a dynamometer car tucked between the locomotive and train, poses for the company photographer at Naperville on January 3, 1944. CB&Q photo.

Silver Arrow, an E5A built in 1941, leads a two-car eastbound commuter train past Eola Tower in October 1949.
Photo by Henry J. McCord.

Opposite and above: One of the Q's mighty O-5A Northerns thunders past Eola Tower with a westbound freight in October 1949. Photos by Henry J. McCord.

To provide backup for the diesel-powered *Zephyrs,* workers at the West Burlington shops converted an S-4 Hudson to a streamlined locomotive, and then built another one in 1937 and 1938. Both of the fluted stainless-steel 4-6-4s, Nos. 4000 and 4001, were given the name Aeolus, who—fittingly—in Greek mythology was the "keeper of the wind." Along with their shrouds, the locomotives were equipped with Boxpok drivers (main drivers only on No. 4000) and roller bearings and reclassified S-4A. Here Aeolus No. 4001 heads a *Twin Zephyr* through Aurora in 1938. Photo by L. E. Griffith.

The last commuter train of the evening gets ready to head for Chicago from the platform at Aurora. CB&Q photo by A. M. Rung.

Prior to placing the new *California Zephyr* into service in March 1949, the Burlington conducted extensive brake tests on the main line near Plano, Illinois. Here new F3s 9960A, B, and C pause with 11 cars between tests. Photo by L. E. Griffith.

The section crew is paying close attention to what appears to be a hotbox on one of the *Advance Flyer's* baggage cars as it cruises at 90 mph through Somonauk, Illinois, on June 15, 1947. The Chicago-to-Lincoln train operated from 1941 until late 1947, when the *Nebraska Zephyr* began service. Photo by L. E. Griffith, Jim Seacrest collection.

Kicking up a cloud of dust as they race westward at 80 mph, a pair of E5s lead the *Exposition Flyer* under a signal bridge between Somonauk and Leland. Searchlight signals replaced the lower-quadrant semaphores on this line in 1942. Photo by L. E. Griffith.

A portrait of a man in complete control: the engineer of a *Zephyr* at the throttle of an E unit, cruising Everywhere West at 90 miles an hour. Photo by William A. Akin, August 1955.

Mendota Tower stood in the southeast corner of the Burlington's junction with the Illinois Central in Mendota, Illinois. Here Northern No. 5634 thunders across the diamonds on a cold morning in the 1950s. Photo by Jim Shaughnessy.

The Mendota Tower operator hoops up orders to the conductor of a westbound freight in 1954.
Photo by Philip R. Hastings.

The engineer aboard 4-8-4 No. 5621 eases his train into motion at Mendota in 1954. Photo by Philip R. Hastings.

Laying a plume of smoke across the Illinois countryside, a westbound freight rolls out of Zearing in the late 1950s. Photo by Jim Shaughnessy.

Burlington E5 No. 9911A, the Silver Pilot, leads the *Nebraska Zephyr* across Big Bureau Creek Bridge at Princeton, Illinois, in July 1948. The Chicago-to-Lincoln train began service on November 16, 1947, with the articulated equipment originally used on the *Twin Zephyrs*. CB&Q photo.

Galesburg, Illinois, was an important junction point for the Burlington. Along with the Chicago-to-Denver main, additional lines radiated north to Savanna, Ill., and the Twin Cities; south to the coalfields around Centralia, Ill.; and southwest through Quincy, Ill., to St. Louis and Kansas City, Missouri. Photo by Henry J. McCord.

The westbound *Exposition Flyer,* led by A-B-A passenger F3 set No. 9960, pauses at the Galesburg depot as a freight rolls through behind grayback F3 No. 132. Photo by Robert Milner, December 12, 1948.

Switching chores completed, this eastbound freight will be rolling eastward out of Galesburg toward Chicago as soon as the air is pumped up. Photo by Jim Shaughnessy, 1957.

A hostler tops off the sandbox on 4-8-4 No. 5634 at Galesburg in January 1955. Photo by Philip A. Weibler.

Class M-4A 2-10-4 No. 6325 and GP7 No. 202 rest on a quiet evening at Galesburg in November 1957. Photo by Bruce Meyer.

The lineup at Galesburg on this day in 1953 includes a pair of E7s leading a local to Chicago; the *California Zephyr;* an E5 heading a local to St. Paul; and an E8 on the point of the *Nebraska Zephyr.* Photo by Kenneth DeSollac.

Shovelnose diesel No. 9907A, the Silver Knight, is in charge of the first section of the eastbound *Denver Zephyr* as it pauses at Galesburg in the early 1940s. Photo by Henry J. McCord.

Class O-5A Northern No. 5634 speeds westbound out of Galesburg in the mid-1950s. Photo by Jim Shaughnessy.

A pair of black-and-gray EMD GP7s leads an eastbound freight out of Monmouth, Illinois, on August 25, 1956.
Photo by Clyde D. Johnson.

A westbound passenger train crosses the Mississippi River into Burlington, Iowa, in August 1955. The span just behind the locomotive swings open to allow passage of river traffic. Photo by William A. Akin.

The Burlington's main locomotive facility was at West Burlington, Iowa. The same buildings that had built and maintained the railroad's fleet of steam locomotives was, by the 1950s, being used for major and minor diesel repairs. Above, left: On the floor in August 1955, five-year-old F7 No. 163 is being prepped for a new paint job. Above: Looking the other way from above, one finds a motor car being repaired, as well as a 44-tonner, the 163, FT A and B units, E7s, and another 44-tonner undergoing repairs. Photos by William A. Akin.

Aeolus No. 4001 is working hard as it pulls train No. 9 out of the Victorian depot in Burlington in the late 1930s. The structure burned to the ground on January 20, 1943. Photo by Henry P. Kuepper.

Chicago-to-Denver time freight No. 61 rolls into Ottumwa, Iowa, behind FTA No. 114D on April 13, 1960. Photo by J. Parker Lamb, Jr.

Here's what the fireman of train 61 saw looking back as the five F units of his train ground upgrade at 30 miles an hour near Woodburn, Iowa, in April 1960. Photo by J. Parker Lamb, Jr.

Shovelnose No. 9904, Pegasus, is leading an E5 on No. 12 about a mile east of Red Oak, Iowa, in the late 1940s.
Photo by Bernard Corbin.

Silver Clipper and Silver Swift, E5s built in 1941, head No. 12 eastward out of Red Oak as No. 7, the Chicago–Denver mail train, passes in the background. Photo by Bernard Corbin, April 4, 1945; Corbin-Wagner collection.

Class S-4A Hudson No. 3007 leads eastbound train No. 6, the *Aristocrat,* through Red Oak at 65 mph on August 6, 1939. Baldwin built 12 of the big 4-6-4s in 1930, and they were the primary power for the Burlington's crack passenger trains into the 1940s. Photo by Bernard Corbin.

Cruising at an easy 85 mph, the eastbound *Nebraska Zephyr* splits the signals on the Centralized Traffic Controlled line three miles west of Red Oak. Photo by Bernard Corbin.

Wartime traffic is picking up as No. 5601, a class O-5 4-8-4 built by Baldwin in 1930, leads a westbound freight near Red Oak, Iowa, on July 28, 1942. Photo by Bernard Corbin; Corbin-Wagner collection.

One of the CB&Q's General Electric 44-tonners leads a short ballast train west of Red Oak.
Photo by Henry J. McCord.

This unusual truck-fed coaling station was a landmark at Hastings, Iowa. Trucks loaded with coal had to back up the ramp and dump their loads into the above-track bunkers. By the mid-1940s, with the arrival of diesels such as FT No. 108, the distinctive structure was living on borrowed time. Photo by Bill Phillips; Corbin-Wagner collection.

No. 6325, a class M-4A 2-10-4, smokes it up westbound out of Hastings, Iowa, in 1945.
Photo by Bernard Corbin; Corbin-Wagner collection.

No. 9137, an Electro-Motive SW1 built in 1939, assembles a cut of piggyback cars
at Council Bluffs, Iowa, in April 1960. Photo by J. Parker Lamb.

The *Silver Streak Zephyr* heads east across the Missouri River bridge from Omaha to Council Bluffs. In 17 miles, at Pacific Junction, the train (which originated in Lincoln) will leave the Chicago-to-Denver main and take the Burlington line that follows the river to Kansas City. Photo by Bob Borcherding, August 1949.

An eastbound freight behind an A-B-B-A set of F3s eases past some heavyweight head-end cars at the Burlington depot in Omaha. The train sheds of Omaha Union Station are visible on the right. Photo by Donald Sims, June 19, 1950.

Steam double-heading with a diesel: An EMD Geep is cut in behind an O-5B Northern at Omaha Union on June 16, 1955. Photo by Bernard Corbin; Corbin-Wagner collection.

Extra 5350 West, behind one of the Burlington's class O-3 Mikados, rolls past F Street in Omaha on June 5, 1949.
Photo by William Kratville.

The wide-open prairie of Nebraska is apparent in this view of a westbound freight rolling through Waverly in August 1955. Note the CB&Q Buick automobile equipped with rail wheels on the road to the right of the locomotive. Photo by William A. Akin.

Denver-bound train No. 3, with several express boxcars and reefers tucked behind the locomotive, pauses for a crew change in Lincoln, Nebraska, on April 20, 1945. Class O-5A 4-8-4 No. 5624 is in charge. Photo by George J. Franklin.

Branch and secondary passenger runs were often covered by doodlebugs such as No. 9767, shown here with a coach trailing at Lincoln, Nebraska, on August 11, 1960. The motor car, an EMC-Pullman product of 1930, had just replaced the *Pioneer Zephyr* on trains 15 and 16 between Lincoln and St. Joseph, Missouri. It was painted silver to match its regular trailer-coach, Silver Pendulum, an experimental car of 1942. Photo by Jim Seacrest.

The *Nebraska Zephyr* prepares for its morning departure from the platform at Lincoln. Photo by William A. Akin, August 1955.

Four-year-old SD9 No. 436 pauses for fuel and a crew change at Lincoln in 1961. The EMD is pulling a train of 15 Atomic Energy Commission cars plus a security crew car. Photo by Jim Seacrest.

In the twilight of a long career, class O-1A Mikado No. 5132 goes for a spin on the Lincoln turntable in August 1955. In less than two years the 33-year-old 2-8-2 will be retired. Photo by William A. Akin.

The wash rack at Lincoln takes the road grime off F3 No. 130D in August 1955. Photo by William A. Akin.

Freight cars coast down the hump at the Burlington's classification yard in Lincoln. Construction of the hump yard began in June 1943, and the first car rolled down on March 24, 1944. Photo by William A. Akin, August 1955.

Lincoln was a busy division point, with lines going east to Chicago, west to Denver, northwest to Billings, Montana, and southeast to Kansas City. Here Class O-5B No. 5627 heads toward its train in August 1955.
Photo by William A. Akin.

The Burlington had been quite active in piggyback since the early 1940s and had several end-loading ramps across the system, including this one at Lincoln. The modified truck tractor was designed to make it easy to back trailers along a string of flatcars. Photo by William A. Akin.

The Burlington's Havelock Shops at Lincoln were the railroad's main carbuilding and repair facility. These photos show the shop crews hard at work in the midst of assembling a run of National Car Co. plug-door reefers in August 1955. Photos by William A. Akin.

The *Pioneer Zephyr* poses with brand-new diesel No. 100, the Q's first four-unit (A-B-B-A) Electro-Motive FT freight locomotive, at McCook, Nebraska, on January 4, 1944. The War Production Board had granted the locomotives to the Burlington to help with the record traffic moved during World War II. CB&Q photo.

Operations along the western Nebraska and Colorado portion of the main line were controlled by the dispatcher via this Centralized Traffic Control board at McCook. Photo by William A. Akin, August 1955.

Grain and livestock were major sources of traffic for the Burlington on Lines West. The 40-foot boxcar was the primary method of hauling grain through the 1950s.
Photos by William A. Akin, August 1955.

The Burlington had dozens of branch lines across Nebraska and northern Kansas. Typical of these was the line to Oberlin, Kansas, where 4-4-2 No. 2564 prepares to leave town after switching the elevator on a pleasant day in June 1952. Photo by Richard Steinheimer.

Nearly new E5 No. 9910A, the Silver Speed, is living up to its name as it sails eastbound with the *Exposition Flyer* near Keenesburg, Colorado, on July 24, 1940. The *Exposition Flyer* began service in 1939 and was named for the Golden Gate International Exposition, held in San Francisco that year. It was the Q's premier train between Chicago and the West Coast until the *California Zephyr* began service in 1949. Photo by Joseph Schick.

The Northerns saw occasional service on passenger trains as well as freights. Here class O-5A No. 5624 rolls train No. 9 west of Hudson, Colorado, on Feb. 9, 1941. Photo by Richard Kindig; Hol Wagner collection.

DENVER

It's a bleak winter day in January 1949 as F3 No. 116 rolls a westbound freight across the Union Pacific diamonds at Sand Creek, just outside of Denver. Photo by Ross B. Grenard, Jr.

Three-month-old E5s 9912A and 9912B—the Silver Meteor and Silver Comet—roll eastward with the *Denver Zephyr* out of the train's namesake city on June 15, 1940. Photo by Richard Kindig; Hol Wagner collection.

Spotless shovelnose No. 9907A, Silver Knight, with B unit 9907B, Silver Princess, poses with the *Denver Zephyr* at Denver Union Station on July 25, 1937. Photo by Richard Kindig.

Denver Zephyr Pullman and coach passengers had no doubt which way to go to catch the train at Denver Union Station. Union Switch & Signal photo, 1937.

Pacific No. 2804, on a rescue mission, brings the *Denver Zephyr* into the station at Denver after a water pump failure halted the diesels. Photo by Richard Kindig, Sept. 24, 1938.

The Burlington's *Denver Zephyr* shovelnose diesels share space at Denver with the Union Pacific's *City of Denver* streamliner in the early 1940s. Photo by Wm. C. Moore; Rail Photo Service.

California Zephyr F3 diesel set No. 9960 gets sand, fuel, and water at the Denver diesel shops on July 23, 1949.
Photo by L. O. Merrill.

Number 133, an A-B-B-A set of Phase IV F3s, awaits its next assignment at Denver on June 26, 1949.
Photo by Earl Cochran.

These two views provide a look inside the Denver diesel shops in August 1955. The photo at left shows E5 No. 9911A, about to become Fort Worth & Denver No. 9982A, and Colorado & Southern E5 No. 9950A. The 9911A was the only E5 saved from the scrapper's torch, and today it runs on the Illinois Railway Museum at Union, Illinois, with one of the articulated *Nebraska Zephyr* train sets. The photo above shows *Cal Zephyr* passenger F3 No. 9962C and a pair of E5s. Photos by William A. Akin.

Crowds line up to tour the Burlington *Zephyr* at Albany, New York, on April 28, 1934. More than two million people visited the train as it toured the country during April and May. Photo by Jack Mower.

PIONEER ZEPHYR AND SHOVELNOSE DIESELS

In the early 1930s the Depression was at its height and passenger revenues were down. Railroads were looking for ways to haul passengers more efficiently than heavyweight cars behind steam locomotives, and they were also looking for new ways to attract the public to trains.

The brainchild of Burlington president Ralph Budd, the sleek, streamlined Burlington *Zephyr* was a three-car articulated trainset powered by a 600-hp diesel engine.

The *Zephyr's* exterior was almost entirely stainless steel. The fluting on the sides, the slanted shovel-shaped nose, and the large screens surrounding the high-mounted headlight all made the train look fast even when standing still.

The train's lead unit, numbered 9900, included the diesel engine, a Railway Post Office, and space for stored mail. The second car had 20 seats for passengers, a buffet-grill, and a baggage section. The tail car had 40 coach seats and an observation lounge that seated 12.

The train's name came about as Burlington officials tried to find an appropriate moniker for what they were certain would be the final word in passenger trains. An initial check of the Z section of the dictionary turned up zymurgy and zyzzle, which—fortunately—were discarded. However, Ralph Budd happened to be reading Geoffrey Chaucer's *Canterbury Tales*, which mentions Zephyrus, the god of the west wind. The name stuck with him, and thus the *Zephyr* acquired its very appropriate name.

The train, constructed at the Budd plant in Philadelphia, made its first test run, a 25-mile jaunt, on the Reading on April 9, 1934. After being christened on April 18, the *Zephyr* spent the better part of the next month and a half traveling around the country, playing host to hundreds of thousands of people who walked through it.

The *Zephyr* was then ready for the publicity event that would make it famous. The Burlington announced that the *Zephyr* would make a dawn-to-dusk, nonstop trip from Denver to Chicago—1,015 miles—to kick off the second year of the Century of Progress fair in Chicago.

Attempting this was no small feat. Normal operating time between the two cities was about 26 hours, and the *Zephyr* would have to cut that almost in half. Also, no locomotive had ever before traveled more than three-quarters of that distance without stopping.

On May 26, 1934, the *Zephyr* pulled out of Denver Union Station at 5:05 a.m., an hour and five minutes late because of repairs on a traction motor. The Burlington had scheduled the run for 14 hours, an average speed of 72.5 miles an hour, but was hoping for a faster run.

After a brief run at 50 mph to make sure everything was running properly, the *Zephyr* cut loose, topping out at 112 mph between Yuma and Wray, Colorado, and maintaining 100 mph for a 19-mile stretch.

The train flew past farm fields and through towns and cities, cruising into Chicago and breaking the timing tape at Halstead Street at 7:10 p.m., exactly 13 hours, 4 minutes, and 58 seconds after leaving Denver, for an average speed of 77.61 mph. Not once did the *Zephyr* have to stop for fuel or for water, the nemesis of steam.

The Burlington *Zephyr* entered revenue service November 11, 1934, operating between Lincoln, Omaha, St. Joseph, and Kansas City. The train was all the Q had hoped for, as operating costs were down and ridership was up—so much so that a 40-seat coach was added to the train in the summer of 1935. The train was officially named the *Pioneer Zephyr* on November 11, 1936.

The *Zephyr* fleet expands

The overwhelming success of the original *Zephyr* led to additional streamlined trains. Next in service were the *Twin Zephyrs*, Nos. 9901 and 9902. They went into service on the competitive run from Chicago to Minneapolis–St. Paul on April 21, 1935. The three-car trains were similar to the *Pioneer*, but each train could seat 88 passengers.

The next *Zephyr* in service was No. 9903, the *Mark Twain Zephyr*, on October 28, 1935. This four-car articulated train operated between St. Louis and Burlington, Iowa.

Next in service, on November 7, 1936, were the most luxurious shovelnose-powered trains of all, the *Denver Zephyrs* (Nos. 9906 and 9907). Each 11-car overnight train was powered by an A-B diesel unit. Unlike the earlier all-articulated trains, the DZ trainsets were a mix of stand-alone and articulated cars, including coaches, baggage-dormitory-lounge, diner, sleeping cars, and an observation parlor car.

Quickly following were the second *Twin Zephyrs*, Nos. 9904 and 9905, which began service December 18, 1936. The original *Twins* simply didn't have enough seating capacity to handle traffic. The new trains each had a single 1,800-hp shovelnose diesel and a seven-car articulated trainset.

The last of the shovelnose-led *Zephyrs*, the *General Pershing Zephyr*, entered service April 30, 1939. The train, No. 9908, served between Kansas City and St. Louis. It was led by a 1,000-hp diesel unit that also included a baggage section. The GPZ was the first nonarticulated *Zephyr*—each of its three cars stood alone.

As the Burlington began buying E units in 1940, Nos. 9904 through 9907 could be found operating on other trains and through the early 1950s ran in the general passenger-service locomotive pool. Nos. 9904 to 9907 were all converted to B units in 1951, serving strictly as trailing units thereafter. They remained in service into the mid- to late 1950s.

The three- and four-car articulated trains operated on a variety of short runs well into the 1950s. The *Pioneer Zephyr* was the last of the trainsets in service, working the St. Joseph–Lincoln run until March 1960. The original *Zephyr*, with 3,222,898 miles of service behind it, was then retired and placed on display at Chicago's Museum of Science and Industry. It can be seen there today, looking sharp following a late-1990s cosmetic restoration.

Dignitaries and Western Union messengers share the platform at Denver on May 26, 1934, as the *Zephyr* prepares for its 1,015-mile, dawn-to-dusk run to Chicago. The time is 5:02 a.m., and in just two minutes the train will move and break the tape, stopping the clock at left, which will mark the journey's starting time. CB&Q photo.

With people watching from the street, parking lots, and platforms, the *Zephyr* is on the home stretch, racing through Aurora at 6:40 p.m. en route to Chicago on its record run. CB&Q photo.

The plaque on the 9900 commemorates the train's nonstop Denver-to-Chicago run and notes that the *Zephyr* was the country's first diesel streamliner placed in revenue service. Photo by Alexander Maxwell.

The fourth car had been added to the *Pioneer Zephyr* by the time this photo was taken in St. Joseph, Missouri, around 1940. CB&Q photo.

Between the Century of Progress and the time it entered revenue service, the *Zephyr* found time to star in the 1934 RKO movie *Silver Streak*, starring Charles Starrett and Doris Dawson. RKO Radio Pictures photo.

The observation car of the 9900 shows its tail sign, added after the train was officially named the *Pioneer Zephyr* in November 1936. Photo by L. O. Merrill.

The original *Twin Zephyrs,* Nos. 9901 and 9902, paused at many small towns and cities along the railroad before entering service in April 1935. The public's interest in the new streamliners is apparent. Note how the top line of the windshield on the power cars carries straight across the front, whereas the *Pioneer* had a rather beetle-browed look as the large grilles dipped below the windshield line. CB&Q photo.

Zephyr No. 9903, the *Mark Twain Zephyr*, was built for service between St. Louis and Burlington, Iowa. The train is shown eastbound at Galesburg in 1937 while the 9903, without its baggage car, was running as the *Advance Denver Zephyr*. The 9903's power car was named Injun Joe after the Twain character. Photo by R. L. Rumbolz; collection of J. C. Seacrest.

Denver Zephyr power units 9906A, the Silver King, and B unit 9906B, Silver Queen, pose with their train on the main line east of Denver in 1936. The A unit had two 12-cylinder Winton 201A diesels for 1,800 hp, and the B unit had a single 16-cylinder diesel and was rated at 1,200 hp. The shovelnoses on the matching *DZ* set, No. 9907, were named Silver Knight and Silver Princess. Electro-Motive photograph.

This under-construction photo of *Denver Zephyr* shovelnose Silver King shows the side-truss construction used on the shovelnose diesels. Electro-Motive photo.

The *General Pershing Zephyr,* powered by No. 9908, had the last shovelnose diesel built and the first nonarticulated train set. The 1,000-hp diesel, named Silver Charger, has a three-axle power truck in front and a two-axle nonpowered truck at rear. CB&Q photo.

One of the original *Twin Zephyrs* blasts through a snowdrift near Lee, Illinois, in February 1936. CB&Q photo.

The summer of 1957 saw the last heavy use of steam on the Centralia line in southern Illinois. Here class M-4A 2-10-4 No. 6327 leads a loaded coal drag into Centralia. Rail Photo Service photo.

OTHER BURLINGTON LINES

Southern Illinois and St. Louis

Coal was the main reason for the Burlington's extension into southern Illinois. The route branched off the Galesburg–St. Louis line at Concord, then headed south through Centralia and continued into Paducah, Kentucky.

Centralia was the hub for coal operations, and in the early 1930s the yard there had a capacity of 2,400 cars. Trains ran from Centralia to nearby mines (more than 50 in the peak year of 1930), then brought loads back to Centralia for classification.

Class M-4 2-10-4s along with M-2 and M-3 2-10-2s powered most coal trains into the 1950s, when six-axle EMD road switchers began to take over.

Twin Cities line

The line to Minneapolis and St. Paul left the Chicago-to-Denver main line at Aurora, heading west-northwest across Illinois to Savanna. From there the Burlington followed the picturesque Mississippi River on the Illinois and Wisconsin side, passing through La Crosse and into the Twin Cities.

Passenger trains were the mainstay of the line, with passenger trains outnumbering freight trains through the 1960s. In competing with rivals Milwaukee Road and Chicago & North Western for passengers, the Q touted the picturesque scenery of its slightly longer line by calling it the route "where nature smiles for 300 miles."

A look inside the Beardstown, Illinois, enginehouse in 1954 reveals a foreman checking the smokebox of 2-10-4 No. 6327, with a pair of Mikados visible through the door. Photo by Philip R. Hastings.

It's a snowy February morning in 1956 as No. 48 swings off the New York Central tracks at East Alton, Illinois, and gets its clearance for the run to Beardstown, Illinois. Train No. 48 was a local that ran from St. Louis through Galesburg to the Twin Cities. Photo by J. C. Illman.

The northbound *Zephyr-Rocket,* operated jointly by the Q and Rock Island, picks up orders at West Alton, Missouri, on March 23, 1950. The Mikado and caboose at left are heading toward Alton, Illinois. Photo by Dave Beattie.

Local No. 48 arrives in St. Louis behind E7 No. 9929A following its 19-plus-hour journey from the twin cities of Minneapolis and St. Paul, Minnesota. Photo by Dave Beattie.

Having unloaded the passengers of the *Morning Zephyr* from Chicago, the E5 pulls the train out of the west end of the Great Northern depot in Minneapolis. After a quick trip on the nearby wye, the train will roll back into the station as the *Afternoon Zephyr* and be back on its way to Chicago at 4 p.m. Photo by James G. LaVake, June 30, 1952.

The *Twin Cities Zephyr* crosses the stone arch bridge at Minneapolis. The Vista-Dome version of the train had been in service less than a year in this 1948 view. CB&Q photo.

Although coal traffic was important for the CB&Q, the 1970s emphasis on the low-sulfur coal of the West made coal a primary focus for successor Burlington Northern; it remains so for Burlington Northern Santa Fe. Here a train of Powder River Basin coal rolls south on the Joint Line at Larkspur, Colorado, behind new EMD SD70MAC diesels. Tom Danneman photo, December 11, 1997.

BNSF Today

Mergers in the 1960s often resulted in mass abandonment, but this was not the case for the CB&Q. The Burlington was a healthy, vital railroad; in testimony to that, almost all of the pre-merger CB&Q (with the exception of many prairie branch lines) remains intact today, nearly 30 years after the Burlington Northern merger.

Burlington Northern, created on March 2, 1970, was for a time the largest railroad in the country. The BN subsequently absorbed former CB&Q subsidiaries Colorado & Southern and Fort Worth & Denver, and also absorbed the St. Louis–San Francisco. The BN itself ceased to exist in 1996 with its merger with the Atchison, Topeka & Santa Fe, creating the Burlington Northern Santa Fe.

Over the years the BN and BNSF have adapted to changing traffic patterns on former CB&Q lines. Agricultural products remain an important part of traffic, although 40-foot boxcars are gone and 100-ton covered hopper cars now haul the grain.

Gone is the livestock traffic that once played an important role in freight traffic. However, one commodity that has more than made up for the loss of cattle is coal. Coal was important for the CB&Q, but it was the coalfields in southern Illinois that provided the traffic.

That changed for the Burlington Northern in the 1970s, as the demand grew for low-sulfur coal of the Powder River Basin. Hundred-plus-car unit trains now head east along the former CB&Q behind orange and green BNSF diesels.

Another type of traffic that has blossomed is intermodal. The CB&Q operated a fair amount of piggyback traffic for its time, but today's BNSF operates dedicated piggyback and container trains throughout the former Burlington Route.

Amtrak's *California Zephyr* is the lone distance name train remaining from the CB&Q's *Zephyr* fleet. The *Zephyrs*, which had been diminished in both number and train length through the 1960s, all but disappeared with the coming of Amtrak in 1971.

ACKNOWLEDGMENTS

The author would like thank all of the photographers who have contributed the images in this book. However, there are three photographers who deserve special recognition for their contributions.

William A. (Bill) Akin, a longtime employee of Kalmbach Publishing Co., made many trips with the late David P. Morgan, then editor of *Trains* magazine. The two often traveled the country together in the 1950s documenting the railroad scene. Bill's photos in this book are from a trip in August 1955, which resulted in a two-part article on the CB&Q in the November and December 1955 issues of *Trains*. Some of the photos have previously appeared in print, but many have never before been published. Bill passed away in 1995.

Bernard Corbin's books documented the Burlington's operations, especially around his hometown of Red Oak, Iowa. Bernie was an accomplished modeler and well known for his beautiful scratchbuilt O scale models of CB&Q locomotives. He also founded the Burlington Route Historical Society.

Finally, the author would like to thank **F. Hol Wagner Jr.** of the Burlington Route Historical Society for his assistance in providing photographs and reviewing the material in the book.

INDEX OF PHOTOGRAPHS